Mary K. Mathis & Soledad Tanner

Soy Latinarrific!
Pearls of Wisdom for Latina Entrepreneurs

For More Information:
Fig Factor Media | figfactormedia.com
Cover Design and Layout by Marco Antonio Álvarez Rodríguez
Printed in the United States of America

ISBN: 978-1-959989-78-3
Library of Congress Control Number: 2024906721

FIG
FACTOR
MEDIA

Dedication

In a world where challenges often test the limits of our aspirations, being a female self-made entrepreneur is a testament to resilience, courage, and unyielding determination. Breaking through barriers that society might have imposed, these women forge their paths with an unwavering spirit.

Each venture they embark upon becomes a canvas on which they paint their dreams, turning adversity into opportunity. The journey of a female self-made entrepreneur is not merely a pursuit of success; it is a revolution against stereotypes and a proclamation that gender should never be a hindrance to one's ambitions.

In the face of skepticism, these women summon the strength to defy expectations. They demonstrate that entrepreneurial prowess knows no gender, that innovation and leadership are not exclusive domains. The grit required to navigate uncharted territories, coupled with the ability to turn setbacks into stepping stones, defines the essence of their entrepreneurial journey.

Being a self-made female entrepreneur is an inspiration to aspiring individuals, a beacon that guides others through uncharted waters. It's a celebration of diversity, proof that unique perspectives and voices contribute immeasurably to the entrepreneurial landscape.

These women are architects of their destinies, weaving success stories that echo far beyond their immediate endeavors. Their triumphs inspire future generations, instilling the belief that the entrepreneurial arena is open to anyone with a vision and the audacity to pursue it.

So, to all the female self-made entrepreneurs out there, your journey is a symphony of tenacity and triumph, harmonizing the notes of empowerment and breaking stereotypes. As you stand tall amidst your achievements, you not only build businesses but also pave the way for a more inclusive, innovative, and inspiring entrepreneurial future.

This book is dedicated to you.

Table of Contents

Acknowledgments

We wish to acknowledge the strength of our mothers, who taught us to be pioneers of thought, word, and deed. They gave us the fortitude to forge on, no matter what difficulties might face us. Here's to the strength and wisdom of our respected and respective mothers:

Alice Lorraine Mathis and Yolanda Cedeno Cabanilla.

A very special tribute to Donald J. Bezahler, our chairman and benefactor, without whom, Latinarrific would not be here today.

Introduction

Soy Latinarrific: Pearls of Wisdom for Latina Entrepreneurs invites you into a world where resilience, heritage, and entrepreneurial spirit converge. The authors met when Latinarrific partnered with the Network of Executive Women on a groundbreaking research project on Latinas in Corporate America. Mary and Soledad found synergies in working together and recently produced a robust online MasterClass called *"So You Want to Be an Entrepreneur."* They believe strongly in the connection between wealth building, having the right mindset, and the direct relationship between financial wellness and physical health.

As a prelude to this book, throughout their years of working with Latina business owners and communities, Latina entrepreneurs shared their unique stories, each one a testament to the strength and wisdom embedded in their cultural roots. Based on these experiences, they gathered insights, anecdotes, and practical advice. They also curated advice from venerable sources, not all Latinas, drawing on the wisdom from proven entrepreneurs, writers, and experienced advisors.

This collection serves as a guide for aspiring Latina entrepreneurs, offering pearls of wisdom that transcend borders and inspire success. Through the pages of *Soy Latinarrific,* readers will embark on a journey where passion meets business acumen, celebrating the richness of Latina identity in the realm of entrepreneurship. It's not just a book; it's a source of inspiration, a roadmap to navigate challenges, and a celebration of the Latinarrific spirit that fuels success in every venture.

Mastering Wealth Building

The Power of Money

"The skills you use to grow wealth can be applied to making the world a better place. Your success can benefit others."

-- *Michael W. Sonnenfeldt, Founder and Chairman, Tiger 21*

Do you have a dream to own and scale your own business, never worry about money, and build a world where women are financially powerful?

Successful women entrepreneurs learn how to build generational wealth, grow legacy businesses, and provide for their families and communities. This has a ripple effect that impacts not only the founder with a dream, but the team she builds to fulfill it, their families, the institutions that interact with them and the economy at large. It is transformational.

The path to wealth means having the grit, persistence, and courage to fight fear of failure, stretch yourself beyond your comfort zone, forge alliances with key partners and providers, and find (and listen to) mentors and advisors.

It is fine to start by being wildly optimistic to the point of delusion, let others underestimate you, and ignore all those who don't share your passion to succeed. Talk to as many self-made women and men who are accomplished and successful and learn from their experiences and turn them into shortcuts that accelerate your road to financial freedom.

Use your money for power: power to send your child to great schools, purchase a home, save for retirement, give back to your community and follow your dreams. Learn how rich people play the money game and program your personal and professional blueprint to success.

Go for the gold! Remove any barriers to your success.

Get Your Share, Get Your Future

"The biggest risk of all is not taking one."

-- Mellody Hobson, president of Ariel Investments and Chairwoman of Starbucks

Are you struggling to achieve financial independence?

Julie Stav, financial planner, broker, bestselling author, and host of an acclaimed daily call-in radio show, transformed herself into a financial expert and educator and inspirational role model now empowering millions through her multi-media communications platform. Her road to success was not an easy one. Despair and failure loomed over a troubled childhood. She was born in Cuba to a well-to-do family whose lives were totally upended by the Castro regime. Her factory owner father became a janitor in his own factory. Painfully sent out of Cuba by her parents to an orphanage in Mexico she was separated from her family for two years.

Later, struggling as a single parent following a difficult divorce that left her bank account dry, she was determined to make her little bit of money work for her and take control of her finances. She immersed herself in the subject by reading everything about finance and investing, pretending to make an investment with "imaginary money" and then putting what she had learned into practice with her slowly earned savings.

Eventually, Julie Stav earned a stockbroker's license and vowed to share her knowledge, tools, and experience with average Americans, including Hispanics. She built a dynamic platform of money and investment books, financial planning seminars, shows and appearances on radio and television, in English and in Spanish, using smart, sensible everyday language, simple to understand.

Julie overcame her struggles, and her tenacity and perseverance despite a troubled childhood which threatened to doom her to a life of failure and despair, but thankfully her tenacity and perseverance propelled her to great success.

Step into a world where financial independence is not just a dream.

Self-Made: Sole's Story and Her Own Pearls of Wisdom

"Don't buy shoes, buy buildings!"

-- Nely Galán—Entrepreneur, TV Producer, and Real Estate Mogul

What does it mean to be self-made?

It begins with financial empowerment, which is more than just having money. It is a seismic shift of thought leading from a path filled with problems and catastrophe, survival mode and worry. It is finding your inner strengths and setting goals.

Self-made women tap into their ingenuity, recognize a need, and build a business poised to capitalize on opportunity.

Self-made women learn how to make money, save money, and manifest the resources, finance, and mentors to help propel them to success.

Self-made women reap the rewards of the seeds they have sowed, by sharing their transformation stories with others to motivate and inspire them.

Self-made women do not give up and have learned how to liberate their dreams.

Soledad (aka "Sole") Tanner, an award-winning trailblazer, took the plunge to move to the United States from her native Ecuador, learn English, get a master's degree, become a citizen, and land an executive position with a global logistics company where she worked for 20 years. She had a dream to set up her own business and take the risk of establishing a financial management and business consulting firm to support the businesses of women and minorities. Sol believes that by increasing financial knowledge, people can improve their quality of life.

Her pearls of wisdom for those on the path to entrepreneurship:

- It takes courage to start a business. It takes determination and resiliency to build the business. It takes financial knowledge and expertise to make it profitable.
- Amidst the uncertainties, adopt a growth strategy: Visualize your dream. With persistence, knowledge, and expertise, anything is achievable.
- You will have to make choices, and none of your decisions will be 100% perfect.
- Prepare for the unexpected; have a reserve and discipline to save.

Think Bigger! Focus on knowledge and preparation.

Get On Board

"You are not truly complete as a woman until you feel confident and empowered to make decisions about your money. Throughout my career, I have seen how a woman who takes ownership of her financial life is transformed and liberated, and how that, in turn, has a tremendous impact on her children. This is my belief and my personal experience."

-- Maria Elena Lagomasino, CEO of WE Family Offices and member of the board of directors of the Walt Disney Company, the Coca-Cola Company, and Avon Products, Inc.

Do you know everything? Do you have all the answers?

A Board takes some responsibility from having an individual making all the decisions, to a group of experienced people, guiding decisions for the best interest of a business. An efficient Board of Directors provides a variety of guidance: legal and ethical oversight, as well as financial stability.

Start today to appoint your Board of Directors. You don't have to wait until you are ready to take in investors, and do not worry about loss of control.

Advantages of a great Board of Directors:

- It focuses on what you need to be successful
- Can help expand your vision
- Amplify business opportunities by leveraging networks
- Reinforce accountability
- Independently help resolve any conflicts with family members in the business
- Promotes company growth by lending credibility
- Board recommendations can help justify difficult decisions

There is a need for more women on Boards. Companies with more women on their board respond better to change, increase corporate responsibility, and improve cohesiveness and decision-making. Getting on a board of directors requires a combination of skills, experience, networking, and visibility.

Strive to be on a Board. Build your skills, seek leadership roles, network, seek mentors and sponsors, increase your visibility through speaking, participate in conferences and panels, and publish articles.

Mindset

We Become What We Think About

"When you want something, all the universe conspires in helping you to achieve it."

-- Paolo Coelho, The Alchemist

Have you ever wanted to do something, but your "self-doubt" talk stopped you from doing it?

The right mindset will help you recognize when you are questioning yourself and have the discipline to overcome those voices that tell you are not good enough, or you can't do it. The right mindset chases away self-doubt and transforms it into hope, courage, and resiliency.

A person with a Latinarrific mindset is confident and has learned how to tell her own story positively and to her advantage. It starts with knowing your purpose or your *why*. In order to truly achieve your dreams, you need to know your *why*.

In the name of figuring out your *why,* let's take a moment to think about *you.* What does being a successful *female* entrepreneur look like for you?

In picturing yourself as an epic success story and a woman of independent means, what does that future look like to you? How do you see this image coming to fruition? Attach an emotion to the picture. The more pictures you can use to support your vision, the better your brain will receive it.

If money were not an object, and you could do *anything* in this world, what would you do and why?

Keeping all that in mind, think about your community. What problems are you solving? What are the needs, wants, and concerns of your target audience?

Take a moment and write down all these ideas. Putting pen to paper creates an intention and a focus on these images. The outcome of this exercise sets the goal, and we want you to keep this image of an independent, successful **you** in the forefront of your mind.

Be Latinarrific!

Secrets of a Millionaire's Mind

"If you want to be a millionaire, you need to think like a millionaire. The millionaire mindset is what lets you make changes in your life and reach the goals you have always wanted."

-- *T. Harv Ecker*

Have you ever wondered why some people seem destined for success?

T. Harv Ecker's book and platform, Secrets of the Millionaire Mind, has changed thousands of lives by resetting their money blueprint which guides financial destiny.

Affirmations create manifestation.

Here are some of the declarations T. Harv Ecker provides in his book, and on his website that you can use to reprogram your thoughts about money:

- "My inner world creates my outer world."
- "What I heard about money isn't necessarily true. I choose to adopt new ways of thinking that support my happiness and success."
- "What I modeled around money was their way. I choose my way."
- "I release my non-supportive money experiences from the past and create a new and rich future."
- "I observe my thoughts and entertain only those that empower me."
- "I create the exact amount of my financial success!"
- "My goal is to become a millionaire and more!"
- "I commit to becoming rich."
- "I think big! I choose to help thousands and thousands of people!"
- "I promote my value to others with passion and enthusiasm."
- "I am an excellent receiver. I am open and willing to receive massive amounts of money into my life."
- "I choose to get paid based on my results."
- "I always think both." (Instead of either or)
- "I focus on building my net worth!"
- "I am an excellent money manager."
- "My money works hard for me and makes me more and more money."
- "I am committed to constantly learning and growing."

Ditch your old money blueprint.

Why We Can All Be Millionaires

"We are the saviors we are waiting for."

-- *Rachel Rodgers, Author, We Should All Be Millionaires*

Do you dream big and want to do good in the world?

Successful entrepreneurs have an innate desire to realize extraordinary values—not only for themselves and their customers, but society as a whole. Where others see nothing, entrepreneurs who are optimistic to the point of delusional, have the vision to create opportunities and succeed, in order give back to their families,

communities, and contribute on a larger scale.

Wealth can include financial wealth (investments, financial instruments), material wealth (tangible assets), human capital (skills knowledge and experience), social capital (networks and communities), intellectual property, health wealth (fitness and vitality), environmental wealth (natural resources), and cultural wealth (traditions, arts, heritage). These overlap and contribute to an individual's overall well-being and prosperity.

If you believe that success, wealth, and harmonious business relationships are your birthright, you have the makings of a successful entrepreneur.

In the book *Today's Inspired Leader: Stories of Impact, Community and Legacy,* the chapter "Unlimited Thinker" by Mary K. Mathis offers mentorship moments for burgeoning entrepreneurs:

- Find what gives you joy and follow it—joy is not the same as instant gratification.
- If you focus on hitting the rock—you will hit the rock.
- Find good advisors. Surround yourself with people who are smarter than you are.
- The best lessons in life come from experience: someone else's!
- Your good advisors may rain on your parade. Listen profoundly.
- Find some positive thinkers and reinforcements to offer encouragement along the way.
- The right partner can multiply your potential.
- Maintain a sense of humor, in essence, find what makes you laugh in a tough situation.
- If you think you are being underestimated, use it to your advantage.
- Embrace diversity. Diverse teams are more productive and profitable.
- Remember if it was easy, everyone would be doing it.

Take a leap of faith and join the Millionaires' Club.

Getting Psyched for Success

"The research says that being successful doesn't automatically make you happier, but being happier - being more positive - makes you more successful."

-- Shawn Achor, The Happiness Advantage

Are you encouraging curiosity and exploration?

The greatest attribute affecting success is openness to new experiences. People work for praise, just as much as they work for money. Rather than focus on praise for skills and abilities, offer praise for effort, strategy, and persistence to ensure greater engagement, as tasks become more challenging.

Make sure you praise yourself along the way. There is power in self-compassion and happiness. Self-compassion leads to grace.

Facing and resolving challenges makes you a better entrepreneur. It is how you overcome the pitfalls that determine your growth, on the road to financial freedom.

People who feel their intellect and talents are limited, avoid challenges. People who cultivate their natural abilities also cultivate growth mindsets. Fixed mindset people find failure a disaster. Growth mindset people see them as opportunities.

In Alan Cohen's great book *Relax Into Wealth,* he outlines some wealth wisdom builders:

1. Describe a leap of faith you have taken and how it affected you and your life.
2. What step would be a leap of faith for you now?

- Why do you want to do this?
- Why do you deserve to do this?
- What fears or reservations do you have about doing this?
- What does your inner guidance tell you?

3. Is there some item or opportunity calling to you that represents making an investment in yourself?
- How might this be a worthy investment?

Repeat this Affirmation from Cohen:

"My talents, visions, and intuitions deserve care and nurturing. My choices represent my belief and my investment in myself."

Health

Harnessing Energy: Persistence to Go the Distance

"The first rule of success, and the one that supersedes all others, is to have energy. It is important to know how to concentrate it, how to husband it, how to focus it on important things instead of frittering it away on trivia."

-- Michael Korda, English-born novelist and former editor-in-chief of Simon & Schuster

Do you know how to channel energy into opportunities and achievements?

Energy is the frequency of inspiration, creativity, and purposeful action. Do you base your goals on your inner needs, not on what other people tell you should be your goals?

What is needed for success is to look inside and see what you need and what you need to do as an individual to be happy. Often this will look completely different from what you were told you needed by your parents, or friends, or the culture. The next thing you must do is have the courage to base your goals on your inner needs, create plans to achieve them, and act on those plans.

Your body's atoms throw off a frequency of energy in every direction. Optimize your energy and you optimize your ability to both attract what you want and create the movement in your environment, necessary to accomplish that purpose.

Be a magnet.

Fiscal Fitness for Overall Wellbeing

"When you learn how much you are worth,
you'll stop giving people discounts."

-- Karen Salmansohn

Do you think you deserve to be successful?

Financial health and personal health are directly connected.

A self-care practice includes taking care of your finances. Saving money, paying off debts, and investing in your financial future establishes healthy boundaries that enable you to find joy and live a more stable and fulfilled life.

Routine checkups should apply both for physical and financial wellness.

It is up to you to take steps to gain control of your financial health so you can get well, live well, and retire well. The challenge is to learn how to go from financial wellness to financial wellbeing.

Start by surrounding yourself with positive mentors. Surround yourself with people who have a healthy relationship with money and who inspire and motivate you to succeed. Avoid people who perpetuate negative beliefs or engage in unhealthy financial habits.

Rewrite the script of your money story. You are not only the protagonist of your money story, you are also the author.

Burn to Earn

"It's not burn baby burn, but learn, baby, learn, so that you can earn, baby, earn."

-- Martin Luther King Jr.

Have you ever thought of the intrinsic connection between physical fitness and financial success?

One thing that most successful people have in common, is a committed attitude to fitness and exercise. A regular fitness regime can instill in you the fundamental building blocks necessary for achieving success.

It has been statistically proven that people who regularly exercise earn at least 9% higher salaries than their less-active counterparts.

Regular exercise enhances your physical and mental state, which enriches all other areas of your life as well:

1. Mental Strength

Focusing on physical fitness creates space for mental clarity and nurtures the connection between mind and body. Through fitness, you can push past your comfort zone and self-imposed limits and transcend obstacles surpassing what you never thought possible.

2. Discipline

A commitment to your growth includes a regular fitness routine that teaches discipline and consistency. Fitness teaches you to keep at it, and to be patient as you round each corner.

3. Brain Health

Working out regularly improves your brain health and cognitive memory, enhancing your concentration and focus. By integrating fitness into your daily life, you are making your health a priority now and in the future.

4. Boosting Your Mood and Confidence

Being fit naturally makes us happier and reduces stress and anxiety. Feeling better physically and mentally is a surefire opportunity to pave your path to success.

5. Generational Wealth

Keep yourself fit to ensure that those who inherit your legacy know how to embrace healthy practices in order to continue to build the momentum that you pass on to others.

Build a business that will stand the test of time.

The Art of Mindfulness to Reduce Stress

"Mindfulness gives you time. Time gives you choices. Choices, skillfully made, lead to freedom."

-- *Bhante H. Gunaratana*

Do you practice financial self-care?

Entrepreneurship is fast-paced, and success is often measured by external achievements. Financial challenges can be conquered through mindfulness practices. Meditation and deep breathing exercises provide the gift of clarity, improved decision-making, reduced stress levels, and enhanced confidence and self-esteem.

Mindfulness practices build self-compassion which helps to overcome the inevitable setbacks and failures that come hand-in-hand with entrepreneurship. Embracing self-compassion allows you to bounce back stronger, with new knowledge, and greater resilience.

Women entrepreneurs are extraordinarily busy, juggling multiple responsibilities at work and at home, with little time to nurture themselves. When we cultivate mindfulness, in the midst of what might appear to be chaos, we slow down, breathe, center our attention, and sharpen our focus, so we can tackle challenges and make decisions that align with our vision.

Being mindful is the catalyst to innovation and creativity. The invigorated entrepreneur knows how to think outside of the box, embrace the power of unlimited thinking and find new original solutions that act as a catalyst to progress. It also is vital in balancing harmony between ourselves as unique and personal individuals, our family lives, and our passion for business ventures.

Practice self-compassion while you find your passion.

Mary K. Mathis

Mary is a serial entrepreneur and a dual national (American and Australian) who truly knows what it is to be bi-cultural. With over 30 years of global managerial, marketing, operations, and sales experience, she has demonstrated expertise in multicultural marketing, emerging technologies, and integrated strategic communications.

Previously CEO of an international management, marketing, and public relations firm, with offices in the U.S., Australia, Malaysia, and Indonesia, the firm also acted as a venture capital and investment company assisting with international trade facilitation and cultural and technological exchange.

Mary has a special passion for projects that empower women. The companies that Ms. Mathis and her veteran media and marketing team have developed cater to multicultural markets in the U.S. with a strong focus on the American Latina. Early on she recognized the confluence of a growing Hispanic community in the United States, an underserved market of Latina programming, a group representing over

1.9 trillion dollars' worth of buying power, and the importance of minority marketing. The most recent venture she conceptualized is Latinarrific—an inspirational, transformational platform to assist the American Latina to be her best bi-cultural self, with tools and training programs designed to advance Latinas, their families, and communities. A second venture, Hispanalytics, delivers financial wellness content to underserved communities. Hispanalytics licenses bilingual, culturally nuanced social media content as a service to financial institutions.

She is a board member of MetaXChange.AI, a global data clean room technology platform with AI video solutions.

Ms. Mathis lives in New York City and Naples, Florida. She is the author of numerous international publications and co-author of *Today's Inspired Leaders*.

Website:
http://latinarrific.com/
LinkedIn:
linkedin.com/in/marymathislatinarrific

Soledad Tanner, MIB,

Soledad is the Founder and CEO of STC Consulting, a financial and business consulting firm that helps improve the profit and productivity of businesses. STC Consulting is a minority, woman-owned small business.

STC Consulting's solutions are:

- Financial Management, CFO On-demand, and Business Consulting
- Financial Speaking, Financial Coaching and Training

Soledad is an outstanding international consultant, award-winner, and global financial business consultant and speaker with 30+ years of extensive international experience in finance and controlling, strategy and consulting, and performance and metrics in the global logistics and banking industries.

She received a bachelor's in business administration with an emphasis in Management from the Universidad Catolica de Santiago de Guayaquil (Ecuador) in 1995, a master's in international business (MIB) in 2002 at the University of St. Thomas (UST), and a Certificate of Organizational Leadership from Rice University in 2007.

Soledad has been recognized by the United States Congress for her commitment and service to the Houston community. She has received multiple awards: "Houston's 50 Most Influential Women of 2022", by Houston Woman Magazine, "Woman of the Year – Entrepreneur without limits, 2023" by the Texas Ecuadorian American Chamber of Commerce, "Women on the Move, 2019" by Texas Executive Women, and "Outstanding International Consultant, 2019" award by Houston International Trade Development Council (HIDTC).

Soledad has a joint venture with Latinarrific, a mission-driven, award-winning, movement to help aspirational Latinas build legacy businesses that impact families and communities. She also serves as their CFO. Latinarrific and Soledad have produced a bilingual business financial Masterclass called "So You Want to Be an Entrepreneur," designed for *The Moneywise Woman with 7 Steps to Financial Freedom.*

Website:
http://soledadtanner.com/
LinkedIn:
https://www.linkedin.com/in/soledadtanner/

Printed in the USA
CPSIA information can be obtained
at www.ICGtesting.com
LVHW061117180524
780181LV00008B/48